Electrifying Personalities

BY ALISON AUCH

TABLE OF CONTENTS

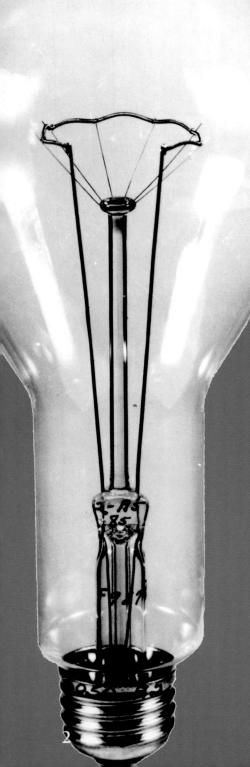

Introduction

If it's dark and you want to read a book, you switch on a light. If you want to listen to music, you turn on the radio. If you want to talk to a friend, you pick up the telephone and call.

If you were living before the late 1800s, however, you couldn't do any of those things! The lightbulb, the radio, and the telephone had not yet been invented. Those inventions—and many more—weren't possible until scientists understood how to use electricity.

In simple terms, electricity is a form of energy that exists in nature. Although electricity is all around us, people didn't know how to use it as a source of energy until the late 1800s.

In the 1800s, scientists began to learn more about electricity. They learned that electricity is related to tiny particles called **electrons**. They discovered that in order to use electricity, electrons must flow through a closed loop called a **circuit**. They also discovered that magnetism is related to electricity and can be used to make electrons flow through a circuit. These early discoveries paved the way for the beginning of the Electrical Age.

On August 14, 2003, a major blackout plunged dozens of cities in Canada and the northeast and midwest United States into darkness. More than 60 million people were affected. Here you can see portions of the New York City skyline before and after the lights went out!

Inventors began to apply some of the new discoveries to their own work. Alexander Graham Bell knew that scientists had succeeded in sending messages electrically over wires as a series of dots and dashes. But the sound of a human voice had not yet been **transmitted**. Bell was determined to be the first to do it—and he was. He invented the telephone, connecting people as never before.

Alexander Graham Bell

Thomas Alva Edison, who is credited with the invention of many electrical devices, is probably best known for the lightbulb. It is hard to imagine the world without the electric light.

Thomas Alva Edison

Around the turn of the 20th century, Guglielmo (gool-YAY-moh) Marconi figured out how to send electric signals without using wires. This remarkable discovery paved the way for the invention of the radio.

Guglielmo Marconi

Much has changed since the invention of these devices. Scientists and inventors have built upon the early ideas and created thousands of devices that define modern life. Although the original lightbulb, the first wireless sound transmission, and the early telephone seem "simple" and old-fashioned, they have dramatically changed our world. Just as early electrical pioneers built upon discoveries that came before them, the creators of today's cutting-edge electronic technology build upon the discoveries of Bell, Edison, and Marconi.

✔ Point

Write About It

Make a list of electrical devices you use every day. Remember that any device plugged into an outlet or needing batteries uses electricity to work. Now try to imagine living in a time before electricity was available. How might your life be different? Write down your thoughts.

In the early 1800s, reading and enjoying a late-night meal were done by candlelight. The invention of the lightbulb would change that.

Alexander Graham Bell
1847–1922

Alexander Bell was born in Edinburgh, Scotland, on March 3, 1847. Bell's parents did not give him a middle name, so he chose "Graham." He often went by that name rather than Alexander.

Bell was born into a talented family. His mother, Eliza, was a musician and painter. His father, Alexander, was a speech teacher, as was his grandfather. Bell himself was such a gifted pianist that he could easily have made a career of it. Instead, he chose to follow in his father and grandfather's footsteps, becoming fascinated by the human voice and human communication.

Alexander Graham Bell made the first telephone call from New York to Chicago 16 years after he invented the telephone.

Bell was an imaginative boy. He went to school from age 10 to age 14 only. Before that, his mother educated him at home.

Bell was not a very good student. He was more interested in pursuing his own interests, such as collecting birds' eggs and animal skulls.

When he was 15, Bell went to London, England, to study with his grandfather. There he met scientists with whom he discussed sound and electricity.

Bell's father had invented a written code called Visible Speech to help deaf people learn to speak. In 1862, Bell and his brothers, Edward and Melville, began helping their father demonstrate how Visible Speech worked. In 1863, Bell and his brothers built a speaking machine. Bell had begun his pursuit to invent instruments for human communication.

The Visible Speech system used diagrams to show how the mouth was shaped when making a particular sound.

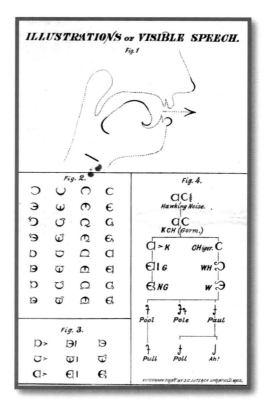

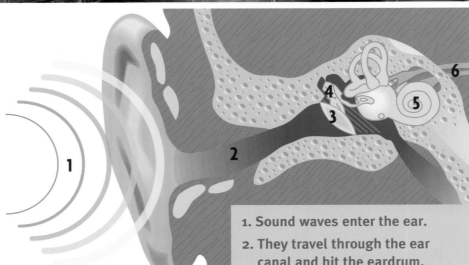

1. Sound waves enter the ear.
2. They travel through the ear canal and hit the eardrum.
3. The eardrum vibrates.
4. The vibrations shake tiny bones deeper in the ear.
5. The bones send the vibrations through fluid inside a coiled tube.
6. Tiny nerve cells in the tube detect the vibrations and send information to the brain.

Determined to Succeed

By 1870, Alexander's two brothers had died from a lung disease called **tuberculosis**. He, too, was sick with the disease. His family moved to Canada, where they believed the young man would have a better chance for survival. Having become a teacher of the deaf in London, young Bell did not want to move. But in 1870, Bell and his parents set sail for Canada.

Bell did not stay in Canada long. In 1871, he moved to Boston, Massachusetts, where he began teaching at Sarah Fuller's Boston School for Deaf Mutes. He was a gifted instructor. He explained to his students that sound is actually vibrations in the form of waves. The sound waves enter a person's ear, where they cause parts of the ear to vibrate. These vibrations are changed into electrical signals that are sent to the brain. In 1873, Bell became a professor at Boston University.

Bell continued to work on several inventions while living in Boston. His fascination with speech had been accompanied by a study of electricity. Years before, he and his brother had tried to transmit the sound of a human voice over a wire.

One of the inventions Bell worked on was a new telegraph machine. The telegraph was the first machine that allowed people to send messages electrically over wires.

Bell hired a young man named Thomas A. Watson as his assistant. One day in 1875, a remarkable thing happened. Bell and Watson had run into a problem. A **transmitter** and a **receiver** on a telegraph they were working with had failed. While Bell was fixing the transmitter, one of its parts vibrated and sent a sound to Watson at the receiver. They realized that they had the beginnings of a "speaking telegraph," or telephone!

It's a FACT

A telegraph machine, which was controlled by an operator, would send a message in code. The code was called *MORSE CODE*, after its inventor, Samuel Morse. The code used short and long bursts of electricity—called dots and dashes—to stand for letters. The bursts went over a wire to a receiver. The operator would control the length of the bursts by holding down a key for a shorter or longer time. An operator at the receiving end would translate the dots and dashes into words, thus creating a message called a telegram.

THIS MODEL OF BELL'S FIRST TELEPHONE IS A DUPLICATE OF THE INSTRUMENT THROUGH WHICH SPEECH SOUNDS WERE FIRST TRANSMITTED ELECTRICALLY, 1875.

It's a FACT

In 1887, Bell met Helen Keller. Due to an early childhood illness, Keller could not see, hear, or speak. Raising her was a problem for her parents. Her father brought her to see Bell, who directed them to the Perkins Institution for the Blind in Boston. There, Helen Keller met Annie Sullivan. Sullivan was an amazing teacher who helped Helen learn to communicate. Alexander Graham Bell and Helen Keller remained lifelong friends. Keller dedicated her 1902 autobiography to Bell.

An Incredible Invention

Bell and Watson continued to work on their new device. Soon, Bell discovered a way to transmit an actual human voice. It was an exciting time as the two inventors continued to improve the design of their telephone.

Bell had to tell people about the telephone and convince them that it worked. He was a good speaker, so this was not a difficult thing to do. The telephone was both fascinating and practical. Although some people doubted that it would ever replace the telegraph, in time it did. Bell's original telephone became the standard form of communicating over distances.

Alexander Graham Bell speaking into his telephone invention

Bell did not stop working after the success of his telephone. He continued his work with deaf students. In 1890, he founded the American Association to Promote the Teaching of Speech to the Deaf. He also made improvements to the **phonograph**, one of Thomas Edison's inventions. Bell called his machine a graphophone. Fascinated by flying, Bell also worked on a flying machine. However, Orville and Wilbur Wright succeeded before he did.

Bell's greatest invention, the telephone, would in time connect the entire world. Bell died on August 2, 1922. Telephone service in Canada and the United States was stopped for one minute as a tribute to the man who had made it all possible.

BELL'S OTHER INVENTIONS

The Photophone
This telephone transmitted speech by light rays.

The Audiometer
This medical tool measured how well a person could hear.

The Aileron
This movable part of an airplane wing helps keep a plane level and control turns. Airplanes still use them today.

The Hydrofoil
The hull of this type of boat skims above the water. In 1917, Bell and his engineers built one that set the speed record for boats at more than 70 miles (112 kilometers) per hour.

Thomas Alva Edison

1847–1931

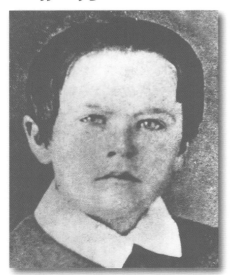

Thomas Alva Edison was born on February 11, 1847, in Milan, Ohio. He was the youngest of seven children, three of whom died when they were young. Because Edison was so much younger than his brother and sisters, he was sometimes lonely.

When he was seven, his family moved to Port Huron, Michigan. Edison caught a disease called scarlet fever, which destroyed most of his hearing.

Edison developed a keen interest in the world and a curiosity about everything around him. This curiosity sometimes got him into trouble at school. His teacher often grew angry with Edison's endless stream of questions. Edison's mother took him out of school and taught him at home. It was at this time that young Edison began to conduct simple scientific experiments—a habit that would last a lifetime.

When Edison was 12 years old, his father's business began to fail. To help his family, Edison sold newspapers and refreshments on a train that came through Port Huron. Whenever he could, he read books or conducted his own experiments.

He had become interested in the telegraph and had built one of his own. When the Civil War broke out, he had a chance to put his knowledge to work. In 1862, there was a battle in Shiloh, Tennessee, in which more than 20,000 men were killed or injured. Edison convinced the telegraph operator at the train station to send an advance message about the battle to all the stops along the train line.

When Edison was 16, he became a "tramp telegrapher." He traveled throughout the country looking for the highest-paying telegraph work he could find. In 1868, he wound up in Boston, Massachusetts, working for the Western Union telegraph company. Throughout this period, he continued to do experiments and work on inventions.

Edison, as a young man, sits beside what was perhaps his favorite invention, his phonograph.

Although this is not an Edison-made stock ticker, it is similar to his. Providing speedy transmission of stock prices was important to the nation's economy.

"The Wizard of Menlo Park"

Young Edison moved to Newark, New Jersey, in 1870. There he started a company that made stock tickers. These machines transmitted the latest stock prices by telegraph and printed them on long strips of paper tape. Edison was paid a great deal of money to find a way to improve the machines.

In 1874, Edison invented a telegraph that could send four messages at once. Up until then, telegraphs had been able to send only one message at a time. This machine helped Edison establish a reputation as an important telegraphic inventor.

In 1876, Edison moved his company to Menlo Park, New Jersey, where he created a research laboratory. There he found himself in a race with Alexander Graham Bell to perfect the "speaking telegraph," or telephone.

Edison lost the race, with Bell's design becoming the standard. However, in 1877, Edison and his research staff made improvements on Bell's telephone. They invented a transmitter that made voices sent through wires louder and clearer.

Life at the lab moved at a fast pace. Edison worked hard and expected his employees to do the same. That hard work paid off. Edison and his team made the first recording of the human voice with a machine called a phonograph. His inventions earned him the nickname "the Wizard of Menlo Park."

The upstairs floor of Edison's Menlo Park laboratory was established in 1876.

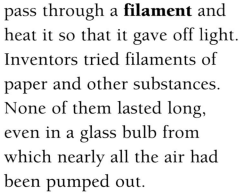

A Bright Idea

Although gas lamps had been in use since the late 18th century, most of the world still shut down when darkness fell. In the 1840s, people began to experiment with electric light. The idea was to have an electric current pass through a **filament** and heat it so that it gave off light. Inventors tried filaments of paper and other substances. None of them lasted long, even in a glass bulb from which nearly all the air had been pumped out.

In 1879, Edison and his team began experimenting with filaments. In October 1879, they got a lightbulb to burn at the Menlo Park lab for an entire day. The next one glowed for 40 hours straight! Soon, Edison put bulbs all over the lab and his house. People came from all over to see this miracle of electricity.

In this photo, Edison holds one of the lightbulbs he made in his Menlo Park laboratory.

Homes and businesses at that time did not have the electricity to power electric lights. Edison knew that his lightbulb would never be more than a curiosity unless he figured out how to make electricity widely available.

He had an idea. He went to New York City to design an electric power station. He and his team worked out a way to supply electricity to a large area. They built an enormous **generator**, a device that made electricity. They ran cables into the city for the electricity to flow through. Then on September 4, 1882, power began to flow from the Edison Electrical Light Company to its first few customers. It worked! Lights went on as planned. A new electrical age had begun.

✔ Point

Talk About It

What are some of the things Edison would have had to understand about electricity in order to invent the lightbulb? Talk about your ideas with a group member. Then write down your thoughts.

This early electric stove, manufactured about 1910, had a separate oven unit. Do you see any similarity to the stove used today?

It took some time before Edison's ideas really caught on. When they did, however, people began working, reading, and writing into the night under Edison's lights.

Edison's invention of a long-lasting electric light was an amazing accomplishment. He had turned an idea into a valuable product.

Despite his success and the fact that he was now deaf, Edison began working again on his phonograph. Although early phonographs did not require electricity to work, more modern and sophisticated versions did.

Edison with one of his first phonographs

Edison's pace did not slow down as he grew older. Although he was now wealthy and famous, he continued to work and invent. He designed car batteries for the Ford Motor Company. He experimented with early movies. He was active right up to his death on October 18, 1931. After he died, President Herbert Hoover requested that homes and businesses across the country dim their lights for one minute to honor Edison. Parts of the country were almost completely dark for that minute. Even the torch on the Statue of Liberty was dark in tribute to a man who had truly lit up the world.

EDISON'S OTHER INVENTIONS

In all, Edison patented more than 1,000 inventions. The following were among them.

A Talking Doll—Edison fit a tiny phonograph inside a hollow doll. The recording played "Mary Had a Little Lamb" when a child turned a crank.

The Kinetoscope—This machine moved a series of still images rapidly to give the impression of motion. It was the first example of "motion pictures."

kinetoscope

Records—Edison improved the phonograph by recording sound on a disk instead of a cylinder.

"Talkies"—By putting his kinetoscope and phonograph together, Edison created the first machine for making motion pictures with sound.

records

19

Guglielmo Marconi

1874–1937

Guglielmo Marconi was born in the city of Bologna, Italy, on April 25, 1874. His mother, Annie, was Irish, and his father, Giuseppe, was Italian. Giuseppe Marconi was a wealthy man.

When Marconi was very young, his mother took him and his brother, Alfonso, to southern Italy during the winter. There he learned to love the sea.

Tutors taught Marconi and his brother, but the young Marconi did not like to do schoolwork. He preferred to pursue his own interests instead. At the age of 12, he was sent to school in Florence, Italy. He was serious and shy, and his teachers were often frustrated by his lack of interest in his studies.

In his free time, Marconi devoured books about science. He liked to tinker with wire and batteries, and take things apart and put them back together. His father thought he was wasting his time, but his mother supported his interests.

Guglielmo Marconi as a young man

Much to his father's disappointment, Marconi began attending the Leghorn Technical Institute in 1887. Giuseppe Marconi had hoped that his son would attend the Naval Institute to become a naval officer.

At Leghorn, a change took place in Marconi. He began to enjoy his schoolwork. He was able to study science. One of his interests was electricity.

At 18 years old, Marconi hoped to go to the University of Bologna. Unfortunately, he did not get in. His mother convinced a **physics** professor there to allow her son to use the university library. With access to the university's books, Marconi began to focus on the idea of creating a worldwide communication system.

Marconi (left) at work in his laboratory with his assistant G. S. Kemp

It's a FACT

In the 1800s, scientists were aware that electricity and magnetism were related. A moving magnet could make electric current flow through wires. Current flowing through wires could create a magnetic field.

In 1861, James Clerk Maxwell determined that magnetic force moved in waves, like the waves that move through water. However, unlike water waves, magnetic waves could travel through empty space. Maxwell suggested that since electricity and magnetism were related, electricity might be made to travel in waves, too.

The secret was to create a wave that was electric and magnetic—an electromagnetic wave. One way to do it was to switch an electric current back and forth very quickly. That switching, called oscillation, is the basic idea behind broadcasting radio waves.

Wireless Communication

Marconi became extremely interested in telegraphic communication. Telegraphic wires had been strung all over the United States and Europe. Marconi wondered if it might be possible to communicate over long distances without those wires. During this time, he learned as much as possible about telegraphs, including Morse code.

Telegraph wires and power lines were strung throughout cities.

One thing that caught Marconi's attention was the idea of **electromagnetic waves**. Though the idea itself was not new, the possibility of using these waves to communicate was.

Marconi began to wonder whether electromagnetic waves could be used to carry messages as a telegraph did, but without wires. Although his professor in Bologna was not impressed by the idea, Marconi was not discouraged. He was fascinated by the idea of wireless communication.

Scientists had already proved that electromagnetic waves could travel very short distances. Marconi set out to get the waves to travel much longer distances—even across oceans.

With his mother's help, he set up a laboratory in the attic of his parents' house. His father reluctantly provided money for the equipment. Marconi spent long nights in his laboratory, working to get electromagnetic waves to travel longer distances.

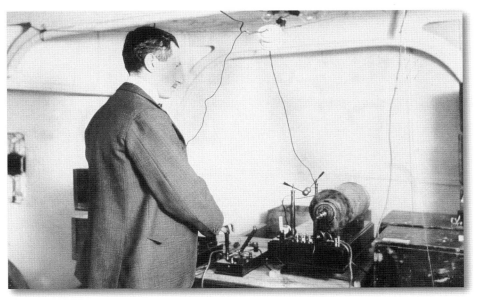

Marconi operates his first wireless radio in America.

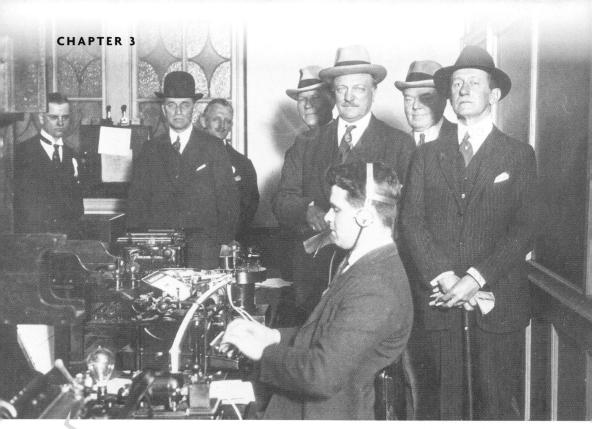

Marconi (right) attends a demonstration of wireless communication at an early wireless station.

Marconi eventually figured out how to send an actual signal—Morse code—across the attic without wires. Soon he was sending messages from the attic to the patio, then half a mile away, then a mile away. He had started a revolution in communication.

To develop his wireless transmission system, Marconi needed more money. His mother's nephew, who was an engineer living in England, offered to help. He knew people at the British Post Office who were interested in Marconi's work. The young inventor went to England in 1896 and began demonstrating his wireless system. It could now send signals for miles. People were amazed. Suddenly, everyone was talking about Guglielmo Marconi and his accomplishments.

The Road to Radio

It was now time to turn a passion into a business. Marconi formed a company that set up wireless stations in England. Progress was rapid. Signals were soon being transmitted across greater distances. In 1898, a ship at sea was able to report news to people on land. In 1899, a signal was successfully sent across the English Channel. That same year, the United States got its first wireless demonstration. In 1901, Marconi and his team battled freezing weather in Newfoundland, Canada, to receive a signal from a station in England. A message had been transmitted all the way across the Atlantic Ocean!

It's a FACT

As a lover of the sea, one of the visions Marconi had for his wireless system was saving lives on the water. At the time, ships in trouble couldn't call for help and were often doomed to disaster. If a ship could be equipped with a transmitter, it could send distress signals and get help.

Marconi, who loved the sea, is shown here with his wife aboard their yacht *Elettra*.

Marconi continued to improve his wireless system. He expanded service across the ocean, and his company grew. In 1905, he got married. Around this time, he began having money problems. His wireless system had still not caught on completely.

Then one night in 1909, Marconi got a lucky break as a result of a disaster at sea. One ship had hit another off the coast of the United States. The wireless system on the heavily damaged ship had survived well enough for the operator to signal for help. Seventeen hundred people were saved. Marconi was a hero!

In 1909, Marconi shared the **Nobel Prize** for Physics. Winning the prize was an impressive feat for someone without a university degree.

It's a FACT

Although the *Titanic* had wireless on board, it didn't work properly and wasn't used correctly. However, because a wireless message from the *Titanic* reached another ship, many lives that might otherwise have been lost were saved.

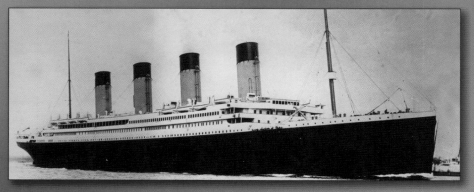

The *Titanic* sank on its maiden voyage on April 14, 1912, after hitting an iceberg in the North Atlantic. More than 1,500 people perished.

Marconi's next goal was to transmit human voices instead of Morse code over the airwaves. At the time, this was called "wireless telephony"— telephone without wires. Marconi and his staff weren't the only ones trying to figure out how to do this. There was a lot of competition. Marconi did not turn out to be the first to broadcast the human voice.

However, he later became the first to get two ships at sea to exchange voice messages.

The start of World War I in 1914 spurred a great deal of development in technology. By the war's end in 1918, almost everything was in place for the first public wireless telephony broadcast—what we call radio today.

Guglielmo Marconi (left) poses in the transmitting room of a new radio station that was set up under his supervision in 1931.

It's a FACT

Guglielmo Marconi was not the first person to successfully broadcast voice over radio. That success belonged to a man named Reginald A. Fessenden. He made the first long-range transmission of a human voice, on Christmas Eve of 1906, from a station at Brant Rock, Massachusetts. His message reached a ship's radio operator hundreds of miles out in the Atlantic Ocean.

Radio became very popular after World War I. In 1919, Woodrow Wilson became the first U.S. president to make a public radio broadcast. In 1920, the first radio stations began broadcasting. By 1925, radio was a major source of news and entertainment in U.S. homes.

Marconi was not really involved in the radio industry. His contribution had been discovering how to send sound without wires, and then creating a worldwide wireless network. Yet the work he did with wireless technology made the radio industry possible.

In 1919, Marconi bought a yacht and made it his floating laboratory. He continued to experiment with his lifelong interest, electromagnetic waves.

Listening to the radio was popular entertainment in 1921. These three enthusiastic fans might be listening to a favorite music program, news report, or baseball game.

The Northwest Railroad running out of Milwaukee, Wisconsin, installed a radio in one of its cars to provide entertainment for travelers. Listening to music, stories, and news was a welcome break from watching scenery for these travelers in 1922.

In his later years, Marconi suffered from bad health. He wasn't able to work much of the time. On July 20, 1937, this amazing inventor died at the age of 63. His death was reported around the world over the wireless network. That network was then briefly shut down—as telephones were for Bell and lights were for Edison—to mark the end of a life that significantly changed communication and the world forever.

Conclusion

Inventors build new ideas from the work of those who precede them. Before Alexander Graham Bell, Thomas Alva Edison, and Guglielmo Marconi invented their breakthrough devices, many others had conducted important research in the study of electricity. Without that information, the lightbulb, telephone, and wireless communication would not have come into being.

Basic ideas about the nature of electricity and ways to harness it were essential to the pioneering work of Bell, Edison, and Marconi. Their imagination and determination made their inventions possible. Their work changed people's lives

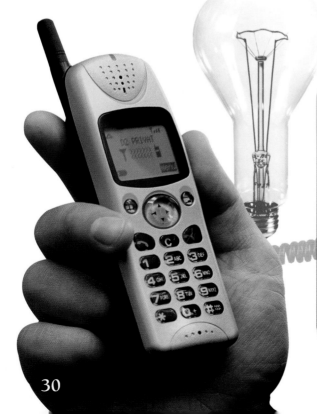

✔ Point

Think It Over

Thomas Edison once said, "Genius is one percent inspiration and ninety-nine percent perspiration." What do you think he meant? Do you agree with his statement?